SPANISH: THE COMPLETE TRAVEL PHRASEBOOK

The Complete Spanish Phrasebook for Traveling Spain and South America.

+ 1000 Phrases for Accommodations, Shopping, Eating, Traveling, and much more!

by Erica Stewart

© 2017 by Erica Stewart
© 2017 by ALEX-PUBLISHING

All rights reserved

Published by:

ALEX-PUBLISHING

© *Copyright 2015*

All rights reserved. No part of this book may be reproduced or transmitted in any for or by any means, electronically or mechanically, including photocopy, recording, or by and information storage or retrieval system, without the written permission from the publisher, except in the case of brief quotations embodied in critical articles or reviews.

Trademarks are the property of their respective holders. When used, trademarks are for the benefit of the trademark owner only.

DISCLAIMER

The information provided herein is stated to be truthful and consistent, in that any liability, in terms of inattention or otherwise, by any usage or abusage of any policies, processes, or directions contained within is the solitary and utter responsibility of the recipient reader. Under no circumstances will any legal responsibility or blame be held against the publisher for any reparation, damages, or monetary loss due to the information herein, either directly or indirectly. Respective authors hold all rights not held by publisher.

Note from the Author

Traveling is one of the most enriching experiences, on so many levels. Being able to interact with the locals makes that experience even more enriching, allowing you to connect with new and interesting people, or even live or study overseas. Traveling is in essence a journey to become more open minded about the world, discovering amazing new people in the process.

As an educator for more than 20 years, I'm a fan of teaching languages to others. This book does not pretend to teach you a commanding knowledge of Spanish, but is an assembly of the most fundamental phrases you will need when traveling to Spain, Mexico, Argentina, Costa Rica, and so many other fascinating Spanish speaking countries!

Over the course of this book, I will convey enough knowledge of Spanish so that you will be able to read, listen, and interact with people in these countries in a way that will inspire confidence. From here, practice will take you to a new level of accomplishments and a lifetime of enjoyment!

Imagine heading out to Madrid, Barcelona, Buenos Aires, Mexico City or the capital of Costa Rica, fully equipped to interact with the locals! I invite you to read on and begin a fascinating learning experience.

Best,

Erica Stewart

TABLE OF CONTENT

Introduction 5
   Different dialects 5
      Central America 6
      Spain 7
      Argentina and Chile 8
      Peru, Ecuador and Colombia 9
   Cultural Interpretations: the Unspoken Words 10
   The Alphabet 11
   The numbers 11
   Word Stress 13
   10 Important Verbs 13
Greetings 13
At the travel agent 13
   Vocabulary 13
   Asking about facilities and locality 15
   When making a reservation 16
When flying 16
   Vocabulary 16
   At the counter: 17
   At the snack bar 18
   At customs 18
   Changing money 18
   Transportation from the airport 18
Tipping 19
At the hotel reception desk 19
Making small talk 20
Dining out 20
   Vocabulary 20

- Ordering food 23
  - Breakfast 23
  - Lunch 24
  - Dinner 24
- When Eating 25
- **Making Payments** 26
- **Locating a tour guide** 27
- **Communicating your itinerary** 27
- **Traffic and directions** 29
  - Vocabulary 29
- **At the beach** 29
  - Vocabulary 29
- **In a historical area or museum** 32
- **While shopping** 33
  - Vocabulary 33
- **Returns and complaints** 35
- **Expressing Emotion.** 36
- **When Ill** 37
- **At the theme park.** 39
- **Appendix 1 – Common Verbs** 39

Introduction

If you've made the decision to visit a Spanish speaking country this year, you might be surprised that you can put your finger on a whole lot of unexpected destinations. While Mexico is the most populous, with over 100 million people whose native language is Spanish, Spain itself runs second with less than half, at about 45 million. Spain is closely seconded by Colombia and Argentina, with 44 million and 41 million respectively.

Nothing new there, but did you know Jamaica, with about 2.5 million Spanish speakers is only second to Uruguay, which has roughly 3 million? Trinidad and Tobago boasts over 1 million, and significant numbers are to be found in the Western Sahara (almost 400,000), Belize (300,000) and Equatorial Guinea (500,000).

Don't have your plane ticket yet? No worries. If you're from the United States, you can find a whopping 35 million native Spanish speakers and those of Latin American descent. If you don't feel like leaving home, you won't have to go further than Texas, Arizona, California, New Mexico, Southern Colorado; New York City, New York; Boston, Massachusetts; Chicago, Illinois; many areas of the Carolinas; and of course, Miami, Florida.

It is estimated that more than 70% of Latin American households in the United States speak Spanish when in the home. This number is comprised of immigrants who've arrived from almost every country in North, Central and South America and the Caribbean. Between residing in an English-speaking country and frequent intermarriages between English and other Spanish cultures, Spanish dialects in the United States are mixed and varied.

As can be expected, the Spanish spoken in Miami has a Cuban influence; that in Boston has a Dominican flavor; New York City Spanish is typically Puerto Rican; and in Los Angeles, Texas and other border regions, Mexican Spanish predominates.

Different dialects

Why so different? Well, the differences aren't so great that a Cuban cannot understand a Mexican, but because Latin American countries were originally Native American, prior to the arrival of the Spaniards, the Spanish of those countries, by and large, keeps many indigenous words --especially proper names; plants, fruit and animals; local geographic features. Other things that can differ greatly, country to country, are names of foods, transport and places to shop.

In general, Latin American Spanish differs from the Spanish spoken in Spain in its expressions, vocabulary, and at times even grammar and borrows heavily from words English. For example, Spaniards would refer to email by its proper form *correo electrónico*, while Latin Americans simply say *email*.

There are other differences, such as the following:

- **Pronunciation.** It's hard not to notice: Spaniards use a TH sound for the letters C and Z; whereas in Latin America, these letters have an S sound.
- **Different Words. Same Item.** Don't panic. The majority of words are the same, but as mentioned above, differences can be expected in certain types of nouns when Spanish is spoken in Spain and the language as it's spoken in the United States or Latin America. As a brief example: the word for potato is *patata* in Spain, and *papa* in the rest of the world. Spaniards say *autobús* for bus, but the Spanish speaking Caribbean islands use the word *guagua*. Where to buy groceries is most varied: Spain: *supermercado*; Dominican Republic: *supermercado* (large),

colmado (small); Puerto Rico: *colmado* (large), *bodega* (small); Cuba: *bodega*; Guatemala: *tienda*; you get the idea. When in doubt, it's best to use the Spaniard version of supermercado.
- **Vosotros vs. Ustedes.** Both forms are plural for "you," but the verb conjugations for *vosotros* are used primarily in Spain, but also in Argentina, while pretty much everyone else uses the more formal version: *ustedes*.

Spanish is about as homogenous a language as English --which differs locally throughout the United States, not to mention in every other country of the world where it is prominently spoken.

Central America

Pronunciation

In Central America, as in almost all of Latin America, the C and Z sounds are all pronounced like S. The letter S, on the other hand, uses the H sound when located at the end of a syllable or when it is located right before a consonant. Therefore *esposo*, or spouse, would be pronounced *ehposo* in Central America, save for Costa Rica and Guatemala. The letter X is also pronounced like a soft H, except, again, in Costa Rica, making *Mexico* sound like *Mehico*.

Vos vs. Ustedes

In Central American, *vos* is used for the second person singular, while ustedes is used for the second person plural. Vos used to be the more the more is an exception, however, as the *vosotros* form tends to be used familiarly amongst family and friends, while the first person singular, when addressing a stranger is *usted*.

When giving a command, the R from the infinitive form of the verb is dropped formal version and an accent is added to the final vowel. Therefore:

Venir becomes *vení* for "*Vení por aqui*," and *pedir* is p*edí* for "P*edí agua, por favor.*"

Others in Central America use *vos*, but prefer to place *tú* in front of the conjugated verb form, such as *tú cantás, tú sentís, tú podés*, etc.

Common Usage

In Central America, the future tense is not used much. As in English, "going to (do, wear, walk, eat, etc.) is primarily used.

Voy a hacer.

I'm going to do.

Van a usar.

They are going to wear.

Voy a caminar.

I'm going to walk.

Va a comer.

He/She is going to eat.

Additionally, in some countries, the present perfect tense is left off, to be substituted for the simple past tense, or preterite.

Different Words, Same Meaning

In Central America, many words do not have Spanish origins, but are native Indian, instead. You can expect slang, transport and words of produce and other foods to have retain a wide variety of the original native vocabulary --and usage varies from country to country.

Different Words, Same Meanings

In Central American vocabulary, many Native Indian terms will be found for produce and other foods, transport and geographical locations, and vary country by country.

Spain

Pronunciation

The distinguishing feature of Castilian Spanish is the TH (as in thing) sound that is used for C, when it comes before I or E, and Z when placed before any vowel. Additionally, the letters J and G, when appearing before I or E are pronounced with a slight huskiness from throat. This sound is non-existent in Latin America, where an H sound suffices.

Different Words, Same Meaning

Many differences exist between Castilian and Latin American Spanish. Some examples include:

English	Castilian	Latin American Spanish
beans	judías/alubias	frijoles/habichuelas
peach	melocotón	durazno
potato	patata	papa
car	coche	carro
to drive	conducir	manejar
juice	zumo	jugo
cool (slang)	chulo	chevere

Vos vs. Ustedes

In Castilian Spanish, the second person singular form, *tú*, is used as normal. The vosotros form is used for the second person plural, when used in a familiar sense, and is conjugated using the standard vosotros form:

you (two) walk camináis
you (two) walked caminasteis
you (two) will walk caminaréis

In Spain, ustedes is used for the second person plural, but only in formal speech. It is conjugated using the third person plural.

you (two) walk caminan
you (two) walked caminasteis
you (two) will walk caminaréis

One marked difference between Castilian Spanish and Latin American Spanish is the use of *vosotros* and *ustedes*. *Vosotros*, used only in Spain, is the informal plural form of "you" and the corresponding verb is conjugated in the 2nd person plural. *Ustedes* is the formal, plural form of "you". However, in Latin America, *ustedes* is used for both the formal and informal address for 2nd person plural but the corresponding verb is conjugated in the 3rd person plural form. For example, "*Vosotros estáis felices*" and "*Ustedes están felices*" (You are happy) mean the exact same thing, but the former would only be used in Spain.

Argentina and Chile

Pronunciation
The Argentine dialect is distinctly influenced by Italian settlers, and the Spanish intonation clearly reflects this.

Common Usage
Like Central America, Argentina and Chile, as close neighbors, have much in common linguistically. These two countries also use the typical Latin American usage of replacing the future tense with "going to + infinitive."

English speakers from the United States and Canada follow the same pattern, whereas the standard future tense "I shall" is used in Britain in a similar manner as the future conjugation of verbs is adhered to in Spain.

Britain: I shall be travelling tomorrow.
Spain: *Viajaré mañana.*

United States: I'm going to travel tomorrow.
Latin America: *Voy a viajar mañana.*

In Chile, the actual future tense is used not for certainty of future action, but when conveying doubt about it.

She's returned from the store. I hope she brought onions.
Ya llegó del supermercado. Espero que traerá cebollas.

More Common Usage
Informal speech: double pronouns, imperatives, diminutives.

- Adding the **diminutives** -ito and -ita to nouns is commonly used to add affection (*Jose-Joseito*) or to diminish long waits and other annoyances (*momento-momentito, ahora-ahorita*).
- Pronouns are often doubled and placed before and after the verb. For example, "I'm going to go" is said "*Voy a irme,*" but in circles outside of professional or school circles, "*Me voy a irme*" will be heard instead.
- When commands are given, informally, the imperative conjugation is discarded for the third person singular tense --but only for some of the more commonly used verbs.

    For example:

Verb	Imperative	Usage
Poner	*Pon*	*Pone*
Salir	*Sal*	*Sale*
Hacer	*Haz*	*Hace*

- The possessive form, "*nuestro,*" is rarely used, instead "*de nosotros*" is heard.
- Finally, it is preferable to use "*que*" in place of "*de que.*" This is acceptable in formal circles as well.

Vosotros Vs. Ustedes
In Chile, ustedes is used primarily as the second person plural and *usted* for the second person singular when formally addressing an elder. *Tú* is also used for the second person singular when speaking informally. The *vosotros* form is seen almost like slang, and can be taken as funny, or insulting.

In Argentina, the *vosotros* form is standard for the second person singular and overrides the use of *tú* for the second person and is conjugated the same way as in Castilian Spanish. *Ustedes* is used for the second person plural.

Peru, Ecuador and Colombia

This dialect of this general region --the northern coast of Peru, extending to the south Pacific coastal Colombia and through the seacoast of Ecuador-- is referred to as Equatorial Spanish.

Pronunciation

As in Central America, Equatorial Spanish also converts the sound of the letter S, when found at the end of a word or after a consonant, into the soft sound of the letter H. Also, the Spanish letter J is pronounced as an English H, as well, as opposed to the throaty J of Castilian Spanish.

Common Usage

Usage in this region is equal to other areas of Latin America: repression of the vosotros form, wide use of usted and diminutives. In Colombia, the use of diminutives is more marked than in other areas.
- Instead of appending nouns, adverbs and adjectives with *-ito* and *-ita*, Colombians use *-ico*, *-ica*, and more notably, use diminutives for verb forms as well.
- Diminutives are also used redundantly, sometimes one after another.

Common usage in Peru is also typical to the region: The morphosyntactic characteristics are typical:
- Relaxed pairing of gender and number between adjectives and nouns.
- Excessive use of the pronoun *lo*, and
- Placing the verb at the end of the sentence

For those who are learning Spanish, it is wise to stick to what is referred to as neutral, standard or universal Spanish --a general dialect that avoids slang and other colloquialisms that can potentially offensive if used in the wrong manner.

Those new to Spanish will also find a comfort zone in Castilian, the official dialect of Spain. This is the dialect taught in schools worldwide. So even if it isn't spoken in most households, it will be understood at the least --even if taken to be a little stiff and proper.

But of course, not even the official language language of Spain is pure. From the Moorish takeover, around 4000 words in Spanish still have roots in Arabic.

Cultural Interpretations: the Unspoken Words

As in Arabic cultures, Spanish-speakers (at least those who live outside the United States) communicate indirectly, as speaking too directly is often perceived as being rude. While Spanish learners should speak as directly as possible, in order to be understood, be prepared to do some cultural interpretations of what you yourself hear.

- **Spanish Family Values.** While some traditions have become more relaxed in the modern era, one's family --immediate and extended-- remains at the core of Spanish speaking societies. When there is an urgent need, expect friends and business partners to come second to family.
- **Machismo.** Male dominance has also become less prominent in some countries, in others, it is still very much in effect. An English speaker may find that the cultural difference is minimal outside a home environment, but, if female, will be expected to serve a male visitor within the home environment. Obviously, the differences between feminist and machismo cultures become much more pronounced within intermarriages.

- **Religion.** In Spain, the official religion is Roman Catholicism. Because the Moors ruled Spain for a long period, there remains a tolerance for other religions, specifically Islam and Judaism. In Latin America, Catholicism also reigns, although many are more agnostic than Catholic. Knowledge of other religions is minimal in some countries.
- **Meeting Etiquette.** Shaking hands is pretty much required when being introduced in Spanish speaking countries. Women will kiss each other on the cheek as a token of friendship or good will. Men and women will even hug once well acquainted --although, if you feel uncomfortable with it, simply offer your hand.
- **Communication.** As mentioned before, a general rule of thumb is not to be too direct, especially when asking questions. Focus more on fostering relationships, and avoid pinning people down for answers. Aggressive behavior is normal in many parts of the United States. Some adjustments will be necessary, unless you enjoy getting a lot of passive-aggression in return. Another important note, is that Spanish-speakers tend to stand closer when communicating directly with someone. It's best not to step back or shun this behavior.

Soft topics aside, let's move into the core foundations of the language.

The Alphabet

Spanish and English both use the same basic alphabet with the addition in Spanish of the letter ñ, which is like the ny in canyon.

There will be situations when you need to spell names out for your listener. For that, the names of the alphabet in Spanish are listed below:

a	ah
b	beh
c	ceh
ch	cheh
d	deh
e	eh
f	effe
g	ge
h	hache
i	i
j	jota
k	kah
l	ele
ll	elle
m	eme
n	ene
ñ	eñe
o	oh
p	peh
q	koo
r	ere
s	ese
t	te
u	u
v	veh
w	doble veh
x	equis

y	y griega
z	zeta

The numbers

1. 1 - uno
2. 2 - dos
3. 3 - tres
4. 4 - cuatro
5. 5 - cinco
6. 6 - seis
7. 7 - siete
8. 8 - ocho
9. 9 - nueve
10. 10 - diez
11. 11 - once
12. 12 - doce
13. 13 - trece
14. 14 - catorce
15. 15 - quince
16. 16 - dieciséis
17. 17 - diecisiete
18. 18 - dieciocho
19. 19 - diecinueve
20. 20 - veinte
21. 21 - veintiuno
22. 22 - veintidós
23. 23 - veintitrés
24. 24 - veinticuatro
25. 25 - veinticinco
26. 26 - veintiséis
27. 27 - veintisiete
28. 28 - veintiocho
29. 29 - veintinueve
30. 30 - treinta
31. 31 - treinta y uno
32. 32 - treinta y dos
33. 33 - treinta y tres, etc.
34. 40 - cuarenta
35. 50 - cincuenta
36. 60 - sesenta
37. 70 - setenta
38. 80 - ochenta
39. 90 - noventa
40. 100 - cien
41. 101 - ciento uno
42. 102 - ciento dos
43. 110 - ciento diez
44. 111 - ciento once, etc.
45. 200 - doscientos
46. 300 - trescientos

47. 400 - cuatrocientos
48. 500 - quinientos
49. 600 - seiscientos
50. 700 - setecientos
51. 800 - ochocientos
52. 900 - novecientos
53. 1.000 - mil
54. 2.000 - dos mil
55. 1.000.000 - un millon

Word Stress

Pronunciation is all about listening and imitating what you hear, but when you're just starting out, a few rules can help as well. Spanish definitely has a different cadence than English, so you'll need to know what parts of the word to stress, in order to pick up the rhythm.
1. If the word ends in a vowel, N or S, the stress should be put on the second to last syllable.
2. All other words should have the stress on the last syllable,
3. Except those whose stress is indicated by an accent.

10 Important Verbs

The following 10 words you already use heavily in English, so being able to master them in Spanish will allow you to understand more of what you're hearing.

More or less, these same words correspond to their frequency of use in Spanish.
To be (*Ser/Estar**)
To go (*Ir/Irse**)
To be able (can) (*Poder*)
To work (*Trabajar*)
To speak (*Hablar*)
To say (*Decir*)
To have (*Tener/Tomar/Haber**)
To give (*Dar/Pasar**)
To learn (*Aprender*)
To do/make (*Hacer*)

Appendix 1 gives you the general useage of the most commonly used verbs in Spanish and shows you how to conjugate each.

Now let's get into the phrases you'll need to communicate

Greetings

Good morning. *Buenos días.*
Good afternoon. *Buenas tardes.*
Good evening. *Buenas noches.*
Have a good night (singular). *Pase buenas noches.*
Have a good afternoon (pl.) *Pasen buenas tardes.*
Hi. *Hola.*

Greetings. *Saludos.*

At the travel agent

Vocabulary

Travel agent. *Agente de viajes/ agente turístico.*

Travel agency. *Agencia de viajes.*

Passport. *Pasaporte.*
Identification. *Identificación* (MX: *gafete*, RD: *carnet*)
Visa. *Visa.*
Plane ticket. *Billete pasaje de avión.*
Airline. *Aerolínea*
Availability. *Disponibilidad*
Booking. *Reserva*
Weather. *El tiempo*
Sunny. *Soleado.*
Rainy. *Lluvioso*
Cold. *Frio*
Hot. *Caliente*
Mild/ Temperate. *Moderado*
Degrees. *Grados*
Locality. *Localidad*
Beach. *Playa*
River. *Rio*
Mountains. *Montañas*
Ecological parks. *Parques ecológicas*
Zoo. *Zoológico*
Museum. *Museo*
Colonial zone. *Zona colonial*
Bank. *Banco*
Mall. *Centro comercial*
Outdoor market. *Mercado al aire libre*
Hotel. *Hotel.*
Airport. *Aeropuerto*
Hostel. *Albergue*
Bed and Breakfast. *Pensión*
Resort. *Resort*
Pool. *Piscina*
Cable TV. *TV por cable*
Wifi. *Wifi*
Local call. *Llamada local*
Long distance call. *Llamada de larga distancia*
International call. *Llamada internacional*
Air conditioning. *Aire acondicionado*
Restaurant. *Restaurante*

Room service. *Servicio de habitaciones*
Continental breakfast. *Desayuno continental*
Buffet. *Buffet*
Hotel lobby. *Vestíbulo del hotel*
Hot running water. *Agua corriente caliente*
Balcony. *Balcón*
View. *Vista*
Suite. *Suite*
Bathroom. *Baño*
Bed. *Cama*

Asking about facilities and locality

I want to go where the weather is sunny.
Quiero ir donde el clima es soleado.

We have plenty of sun in the Dominican Republic.
Tenemos un montón de sol en la República Dominicana.

I would like to stay at a beach resort.
Me gustaría estar en un resort de playa.

I would like to stay at a mountain resort.
Me gustaría estar en un resort de montaña.

I would like to stay at a nice hotel in the capital city.
Me gustaría quedarme en un buen hotel en la ciudad capital.

Are there nice hotels or hostels in the colonial zone?
¿Hay buenos hoteles o albergues de la zona colonial?

Which hotel offers free wifi?
¿Qué hotel ofrece wifi gratuito?

Do any have free cable TV?
¿Alguno tienen TV por cable gratuita?

Will I be allowed to make local calls for free?
Se me permitirá hacer llamadas locales gratis?

How much are long distance and international calls?
¿Cuánto son de larga distancia y llamadas internacionales?

Do the rooms have air conditioning?
¿Las habitaciones tienen aire acondicionado?

Is there a restaurant in the hotel?
¿Existe algún restaurante en el hotel?

Does the restaurant offer room service?

¿El restaurante ofrece servicio de habitaciones?

Does the hotel offer free breakfast --continental breakfast or a full buffet?
¿El hotel ofrece desayuno gratis --de continental o de buffet completo?

Is there Wifi in the hotel lobby or restaurant?
¿Hay Wifi en el vestíbulo del hotel o en el restaurante?

I would like to tour the colonial zone primarily, but of course I want to go to the beach.
Me gustaría visitar la zona colonial principalmente, pero por supuesto que quiero ir a la playa.

Does the hotel/hostel have hot running water?
¿El hotel / hostal tener agua corriente caliente?

Will my room have a balcony?
¿Mi habitación tendrá un balcón?

What kind of view will I see from my room?
¿Qué tipo de vista voy a ver desde mi habitación?

Is the hotel far from the supermarket/mall/beach/bank/airport?
¿Es el hotel lejo del supermercado / centro comercial / playa / banco / aeropuerto?

Is there an open market in the locality?
¿Hay un mercado abierto en la localidad?

When making a reservation

I would like a suite. How many beds are there? How many bathrooms are there?
Me gustaría una suite. ¿Cuántas camas hay? ¿Cuántos baños hay?

I only need a single room with a king bed.
Yo sólo necesito una habitación individual con una cama extragrande.

A double room with two queen beds is fine.
Una habitación doble con dos grandes está bien.

Are young children allowed to stay?
¿Los niños pequeños les permite quedar?

I will need a crib.
Voy a necesitar una cuna.

Is there a fridge in the room?
¿Hay una nevera en la habitación?

When flying

Vocabulary

Reservation. *Reserva*
Credit card. *Tarjeta de crédito*
Cash. *Efectivo*
Ticket. *Billete*
Passport. *Pasaporte*
Boarding Pass. *Pase de abordar*
Gate. *Puerta*
Luggage. *Equipaje*
Luggage cart. *Carrito de equipaje*
Luggage weight. *Peso de equipaje*
Carry-on. *Equipaje de mano*
Wheelchair. *Silla de ruedas*
Reservation number. *Numero de reserva*
Security checkpoint. *Puesto de control de seguridad*
X-ray machine. *Máquina Rayos-X*
Scanner. *Escáner*
Window seat. *Asiento de ventana*

At the counter:

Do you have a reservation?
¿Tiene usted una reserva?

May I have your ticket and passport, please?
Puedo ver su billete y pasaporte, por favor?

Here is my passport and ticket.
Aquí está mi pasaporte y el billete.

Do you prefer a window seat?
¿Prefiere un asiento de la ventana?

Do you have any luggage?
¿Tiene algún equipaje?

I have two suitcases.
Tengo dos maletas.

Can you put them here on the scale please?
¿Puedes ponerlos aquí en la escala por favor?

The first suitcase is free. The second will be $75. Would you like to pay with a credit card?
La primera maleta es gratis. El segundo será de $ 75. ¿Te gustaría pagar con tarjeta de crédito?

No, I will pay with cash.
No, voy a pagar con efectivo.

You may take your carry-on, purse and jacket with you.
Usted puede tomar su equipaje de mano, bolso (Lat.Am.: cartera) y la chaqueta con usted.

Here is your boarding pass.
Aquí está su tarjeta de embarque.

After the security checkpoint to your left, you will go to Gate B5. Your seat is A42.
Después de que el puesto de control de seguridad a la izquierda, que se destinará a Gate B5. Su asiento es A42.

Is the gate far? I will need a wheelchair. My health doesn't permit me to walk far.
Es la puerta leja? Voy a necesitar una silla de ruedas. Mi salud no me permite caminar mucho.

At the snack bar

How much is this please?
¿Cuánto es esto, por favor?

Cappuccino, please.
Cappuccino, por favor

Do you accept American dollars/euros?
¿Aceptan dólares estadounidenses / euros?

At customs

How long are you staying?
¿Por cuánto tiempo es usted va a quedar?

I am staying for one week.
?.?.Me quedo por una semana.

What is the purpose of your trip?
¿Qué es el propósito de su viaje?

I am on vacation.
Estoy de vacaciones

How much money do you have with you?
¿Cuánto dinero tienes contigo?

I have $1000.
Tengo $ 1000

Enjoy your stay.
Disfrute de su estancia.

Thank you!
Gracias!

Changing money
*It's always good to ask at the hotel desk where to exchange money.

What is the rate of exchange?
¿Cuál es la tasa de cambio?

I would like to change $700 into pesos.
Me gustaría cambiar 700 dólares a pesos.

Transportation from the airport
Excuse me, Where is/Is this the shuttle for the Hilton Hotel?
Perdone, ¿Dónde está / ¿Es este el traslado para el Hilton Hotel ?

To a taxi driver: How much is to go to the Hilton Hotel downtown?
¿Cuánto es para ir al Hilton Hotel en el centro de la ciudad?

Tipping
*It's always good to ask at the hotel desk what are the proper tip amounts for different services:

How much is the normal tip for:
- the cleaning staff
- a driver
- someone who bags groceries
- a tour guide
- a server

¿Cuánto es la propina normal para:
- *el personal de limpieza*
- *de un conductor*
- *que alguien bolsas Abarrotes*
- *un guía turístico*
- *de un servidor*

*In developing countries, foreigners are generally expected to give a little extra on top of the normal tip, but this is optional.

How it is said:
Are employees allowed to accept tips?
¿Los empleados estan autorizados a aceptar propinos?

Take this, please. The rest is for you.
Tome esto, el resto es para usted.

Thank you for your help. This is for you.
Gracias por tu ayuda. Esto es para ti.

At the hotel reception desk

I have a reservation for today for a double room with a balcony.
Tengo una reserva para hoy por una habitación doble con balcón.

My name is Jill Brandon. Here is my passport.
Mi nombre es Jill Brandon. Aquí está mi pasaporte.

Can someone help me with my luggage?
¿Puede alguien ayudarme con mi equipaje?

How late is the restaurant open?
¿Hasta qué hora está abierto el restaurante?

How late do you offer room service?
¿Hasta qué hora es lo que ofrece servicio a la habitación?

What time do you serve breakfast in the morning?
¿A qué hora te sirven el desayuno en la mañana?

Making small talk

I'm Jill.
Soy Jill.

Nice to meet you.
Encantado/a

Where are you from?
¿De dónde eres?

I'm from Canada.
Soy de Canadá.

This is my third time coming to this country.
Esta es la tercera vez que vengo a este país.

I always stay in this hotel.
Siempre me alojo en este hotel.

I'm here on business.
Estoy aquí por negocios.

What do you do?
¿Qué haces?

I'm a teacher/lawyer/doctor/business person.
Soy un profesor / abogado / médico / persona de negocios.

Dining out

Vocabulary

water. *agua*
black tea. *té negro*

mint tea. *té de menta*
coffee *café*
milk *leche*
cream *crema*
hot chocolate *chocolate*

sugar *azúcar*
honey *miel*
grape jelly *jalea de uva*
strawberry jam *mermelada de fresa*
syrup *sirop*

pastry *postre*
bread *pan*
butter *mantequilla*
croissant *croissant*
eggs *huevos*
cheese *queso*
oatmeal *avena*
toast *pan tostada*
pancakes *panqueques*
plantains *platanos*

fruit *frutas*
melon *melon*
apple *manzana*
pineapple *piña*
banana *guineo (Carib.) banana (almost all)*
strawberry *fresa*
mango *mango*
kiwi *kiwi*
peach *melocotón (SP), durazno (almost all)*
passion fruit *chinola*
orange *naranja*
lemon *limón*
juice *jugo*
lemonade *jugo de limón/ limonada*
orange juice *jugo de naranja*
apple juice *jugo de manzana*

yogurt *yogur*
custard *natilla*
Jello *gelatina*
crackers *galletas*

cookies *galletas, galleticas (RD)*
soda *refresco*

rice *arroz*
pasta *pasta*
spaghetti *espaguetis*
soup *sopa (de)*
salad *ensalada (de)*
sandwich *sándwich (de)*
fruit salad *ensalada de frutas*

rice (plain) *arroz blanco*
rice and beans *arroz y frijoles, Moro (Carib.)*
rice with seafood *paella*
yellow rice *arroz amarillo*
fried rice (Chinese) *chofan*

meat *carne*
chicken *pollo*
chicken breast *pechuga de pollo*
chicken wings *alas de pollo*
drumstick *palillo*
chicken thigh *muslo*
beef *carne de res*
pork *carne de cerdo*
goat *carne de chivo*
lamb *cordero*

fish *pescado*
tuna *atún*
tilapia *tilapia*

sea bass *lubina*
catfish *bagres*
whiting *bacaladilla*
squid *calamares*
calamari *calamares*
shrimp *camarones*
crab *cangrejo*
lobster *langosta*
mussels *mejillones*
clams *almejas*
oysters *ostras*
smoked herring *ahumadas arenque*
saltfish *bacalao*
sardines *sardinas*
seafood salad (raw) *ceviche*

vegetables *verduras*
potatoes *papas, patatas (SP)*
green beans *judías verdes*

spinach *espinaca*
broccoli *brócoli*
green pepper *pimiento verde*
onion *cebolla*
carrot *zanahoria*
tomato *tomate*
eggplant *berenjena*
okra *okra*
zucchini *calabacín*
corn *maíz*
olives *aceitunas*
olive oil *aceite de oliva*
vinegar *vinagre*

salad dressing *aliño*

fried *frito*
grilled (outdoor) *asado*
grilled (indoor) *a la plancha*
stewed *guisado*
boiled *hervida*
baked *horneada*

dessert *postre*
pie *py*
ice cream *helado*
rice pudding *pudín de arroz*
bread pudding *pudín de pan*
corn pudding *pudín de maiz*

plate *plato*
cup *taza*
glass *vaso*
spoon *cuchara*
fork *tenedor*
knife *cuchillo*
napkin *servilleta*
table *mesa*
chair *silla*
patio *patio*

Ordering food

Breakfast
What's for breakfast?
¿Qué hay para el desayuno?

I'll have a cup of coffee/tea, please.

Voy a tomar una taza de café / té, por favor.

What kind of fruit do you have?
¿Qué tipo de fruta tiene usted?

I would like yogurt with bananas and apples.
Me gustaría yogur con bananas y manzanas.

Bread and butter with hot chocolate, please.
Pan y mantequilla con el chocolate caliente, por favor.

I'll have oatmeal.
Voy a tener avena.

Please bring me eggs and toast with butter and jelly.
Por favor, tráeme huevos y tostadas con mantequilla y mermelada.

I like my eggs soft/hard, boiled/scrambled/fried.
Me gustan mis huevos suave / duro, hervida / revueltos / frito.

I'll have a cheese and tomato omelet and fried potatoes.
Voy a tener un tortilla de queso y tomate y papas fritas.

Do you have pancakes and syrup?
¿Tiene panqueques y sirop?
I would like mashed plantains with fried eggs.
Me gustaría puré de plátano con huevos fritos.

Lunch
Barbecue chicken with fried plantains, please.
Pollo asado con plátanos fritos, por favor.

I'll have your stewed goat special with plain rice and salad.
Voy a tener el especial de chivo guisado con arroz blanco y ensalada.

Is the fish very fresh? I would like it fried, please, with mashed potatoes.
¿Es el pescado muy fresco? Me gustaría frito, por favor, con puré de patatas.

I would like the beef and vegetable soup with bread and a green salad.
Me gustaría la sopa de carne y verduras con pan y una ensalada verde.

I'll have pie with ice cream for dessert. Yes, the pie a-la-mode.
Voy a tener el py con helado de postre. Sí, el py a-la-moda.

Chocolate cake with strawberries sounds delicious. I'll have that.
El pastel de chocolate con fresas suena delicioso. Voy a tener eso.

Dinner
A tuna sandwich with fried potatoes please.
Un sándwich de atún con patatas fritas favor.

Eggs with fried cheese sounds excellent.
Huevos con queso frito suena excelente.

A mint tea with bread and cheese would be perfect.
Un té de menta con pan y queso sería perfecto.

Please bring me crackers with seafood salad.
Por favor, tráeme galletas con ceviche.

When Eating

What is it made from?
De qué es hecho?

Sweet. *Dulce.*
Sour. *Agrio/a*
Savory or Salty. *Salad/a.*
I would like bread.
Me gustaría pan.

Pass me the salt.
Páseme la sal.

Dish (specific preparation, or a plate.) *Plato.*

It's very good. (food)
Es muy bueno.

I don't prefer it.
No lo prefiero.

May I sample/taste it?
Puedo probarlo?

Would you like a taste?
Quisiera usted un gusto?

I will cook.
Cocinaré.

We'll eat together.
Comeremos juntos.

Are you a chef?
Eres un chef?

I am in culinary school.
Estoy en la escuela culinaria.

No sugar, please.
Sin azúcar, por favor.

I prefer no fat, or low-fat.
Prefiero sin grasa o bajo en grasa.

Put a lot of sugar/cream, please.
Ponga mucho azúcar/crema, por favor.

Do you have anything low in sodium?
Tienes algo bajo en sodio?

Is it oily/greasy?
Es aceitoso?

Nothing fried.
Nada frito.

Any condiments?
Los condimentos?

What do you have for dessert?
Qué tienes para el postre?

Just coffee.
Sólo café.

I would like to sit outdoors.
Me gustaría sentarme al aire libre/en el patio.

I prefer to sit somewhere quiet.
Prefiero sentarme en algún lugar tranquilo.

We are a party of 10.
Somos un grupo de 10.

Where is the bathroom?
Dónde está el baño?

What dish is the restaurant specialty?
Qué plato es la especialidad del restaurante?

Do you have any specials?
Hay ofertas especiales?

What is the Plate of the Day?
Cuál es el plato del día?

Please bring extra napkins.
Por favor, traiga servilletas extras.

Chinese/Spanish/Venezuela/Arabic/Indian/Italian Food
Comida china/ española/ venezolana/ árabe/ india/ italiana

Making Payments

How it is said:
How much do I owe you?
¿Cuánto te debo?

The bill, please.
La cuenta, por favor.

I would like a receipt.
Me gustaría un recibo.

Do you accept American dollars/euros?
¿Se aceptan dólares estadounidenses / euros?

What is your rate of exchange?
¿Cuál es su tasa de cambio?

Do you charge extra fees to bill a foreign card?
¿Cobran cargos extra para facturar una tarjeta extranjera?

Do you accept Visa/Mastercard?
¿Se aceptan Visa / Mastercard?

Is tax included in the meal?
¿Es el impuesto incluido en la comida?

Locating a tour guide

The hotel desk staff should be happy to point you in the right direction here, as well:

How it is said:
Do you know of a reliable tour guide?
¿Conoce un guía confiable?

Communicating your itinerary

(See **At the travel agent, Vocabulary**)
I'm here for ___ days.
Estoy aquí por ___ días.

In that time, I would like to:
1. Go to the beach
2. See the old cathedrals
3. Shop for souvenirs
4. Eat at a good local restaurant

    5.   Try local fruit
    6.   Go to the museums
    7.   Drive through some of the neighborhoods
    8.   Drive through the mountains and see the rivers
    9.   See the colonial zone

En ese tiempo, me gustaría:
    1.   *Ir a la playa*
    2.   *Ver las viejas catedrales*
    3.   *tienda de recuerdos*
    4.   *comer a un buen restaurante local*
    5.   *Trate fruta local*
    6.   *Ir a los museos*
    7.   *Conduzca a través de algunos de los barrios*
    8.   *Conduzca a través de las montañas y ver los ríos*
    9.   *Ver la zona colonial*

How it is said:

What is your transportation like?
¿Como es su transporte?

Do you know where we can find these things?
¿Sabes dónde podemos encontrar estas cosas?

How much will you charge per day?
¿Cuánto va a cobrar por día?

How many people can come with us?
¿Cuántas personas pueden venir con nosotros?

Where is the vegetable market?
¿Dónde está el mercado de verduras?

Is there a corner store nearby?
¿Hay un colmado cerca?

Do they deliver?
¿Tienen servicio domicilio?

I'm going shopping.
Voy de compras.

I'm going to the supermarket.
Voy al supermercado.

I'll take five of them.
Tomaré a cinco de ellos. (OR *Me quedo con cinco de ellos.*)

Just one, please.
Uno sólo por favor.

Was this made today?

¿Esto fue hecho hoy?

Traffic and directions

Vocabulary

Left – *Izquierda*
Right – *Derecha*
Go alon/Continue - *Sigue*
To cross the street - *Cruzar la calle*
Across the street - *A través de la calle*
Near – *Cercano(a), próximo(a)*
Next to – *Al lado de*
Between – *Entre*
At the end (of) – *Al final (de)*
On/at the corner – *En la esquina*
Behind – *Detrás de*
In front of – *En frente de*
Around the corner – *A la vuelta de la esquina*
Traffic light – *El semáforo*
crossroads – *El cruce*
Signpost – *La señal*

At the beach

Vocabulary

Beach. *Playa*
Waterfront. *Malecon*
River. *Rio*
Lake. *Lago*
Swimsuit. *Traje de baño*
Swim trunks. *Troncos*
Water shoes. *Zapatos de agua*
Goggles. *Gafas*
Lifesaver. *Salvadora*
Life jacket. *Chaleco salvavidas*
Tube. *Tubo*
Flippers. *Aletas*
Water. *Agua*
Wave. *Ola*
Big wave. *Ola grande*
Tide. *Marea*
Sand. *Arena*
Rocks. *Rocas*
Sand castle. *Castillo de la arena*
Shell. *Concha*
Fish. *Pescado*
Shark. *Tiburón*

Ocean. *Océano*
Sea. *Mar*
Shallow water. *Aguas superficiales*
Deep water. *Aguas profundas*
Calm waters. *Aguas tranquilas*
Rough waters. *Aguas bravas*
Safe area. *Zona segura*
To swim. *Nadar*
Float. *Flotar*
Picnic. *Picnic*
Wet. *Mojado/a*
Towel. *Toalla*
To dry oneself. *Secar a sí mismo*
Dry. *Seco*
Full of sand. *Lleno de arena*
To rest oneself. *Descansarse*
To tan oneself. *Broncearse*
Sunscreen. *Protector solar*
Lounge chair. *Silla de salón*
Sun. *Sol*
To jump. *Saltar*
Canoe. *Canoa*
Surfboard. *Tabla de Surf*
Yacht. *Yate*
Water ski. *Esquí acuático*
To snorkel. *Bucear*

How it is said:
Let's go to the beach.
Vamos a la playa.

I want to go swimming.
Quiero ir a nadar.

Did you bring your swimsuit/trunks?
¿Trajiste tu traje de baño / troncos?

I can't swim.
No sé nadar

I can float in the sea all day long.
Puedo flotar en el mar durante todo el día.

I'm just going to get a tan.
Yo sólo voy a tomar el sol.

Do you have sunscreen?
¿Tiene protector solar?

The sun is very strong here.
El sol es muy fuerte aquí.

Do those markers indicate a safe area for swimming?
¿Esos marcadores indican una zona segura para nadar?

I swim like a fish.
Nado como un pez.

Here comes a wave!
Aquí viene una ola!

It's a big wave. Jump!
Es una gran ola. Jump!

Please wear a life jacket.
Por favor, use un chaleco salvavidas.

I'll hang on to this life saver.
Voy a colgar a este protector de la vida.

Do you have a tube?
¿Tiene un tubo?

Do they rent canoes or surfboards?
¿Se alquilan canoas o tablas de surf?

Can we water ski there?
¿Podemos esquí acuático allí?

I'd like to go snorkeling.
Me gustaría ir a bucear.

Are any yachts/boats available?
¿Hay yates / barcos disponibles?

These are rough waters.
Estas son aguas turbulentas.

The water is calm. A baby can swim here.
El agua está en calma. Un bebé puede nadar aquí.

Is this whole area shallow?
¿Es todo este poco profunda zona?

There is a sudden drop into deep waters.
Hay una caída repentina en aguas profundas.

The river/lake/sea is shallow all the way to the other side.
El río / lago / mar es poco profundo todo el camino hasta el otro lado.

I can only swim in deep water.
Sólo puedo nadar en aguas profundas.

I brought my flippers/goggles/snorkel.
Me llevé a mis aletas / gafas / snorkel.

The rocks on the bottom can be sharp. I'll wear water shoes.
Las rocas en la parte inferior puede ser agudo. Voy a usar zapatos de agua.

Are there fish?
¿Hay peces?

Are there sharks?
¿Hay tiburones?

I need to rest a bit.
Necesito descansar un poco.

This sand is very fine.
Esta arena es muy fina.

I think I'll build a sandcastle.
Creo que voy a construir un castillo de arena.

If you see any shells, give them to me. I'm shell-hunting.
Si hay conchas, les dan a mí. Estoy en caza de concha.

The tide is out/in.
La marea está baja / en.

In a historical area or museum

How it is said:
Are there any traces of Moorish/Islamic culture remaining here?
¿Hay rastros de mora / cultura islámica restantes aquí?

I hear Spanish colonialists occupied this city heavily. Have any of these homes been preserved inside?
Oigo colonialistas españoles ocuparon esta ciudad en gran parte. ¿Alguno de estos hogares han conservado dentro?

I would like to see the layout of the homes and get a feel for how they lived.
Me gustaría ver la distribución de los hogares y tener una idea de cómo vivían.

I hear Moroccan floor tiles were much in use.
Oigo baldosas marroquíes eran mucho en uso.

Is this where the Indian artifacts of the local tribes can be viewed?
Es aquí donde los artefactos indios de las tribus locales pueden ser miraba?

I would like to visit the old town/ colonial zone.
Me gustaría visitar el casco antiguo de zona / colonial.

This is a huge tomb! Who is buried here?
Esta es una gran tumba! ¿Quién está enterrado aquí?

What do the flags signify?
¿Qué significan las banderas?

From the local food and facial features of many of the people, they seem to be descendants of Indians/Africans/ Spanish/French.
De la comida local y las características faciales de muchas de las personas, parecen ser descendientes de los indios/africanos/español/francés.

These nuns/ priests dress differently from the way I normally see them back home. What order do they belong to?
Estas monjas / sacerdotes se visten de manera diferente a lo que normalmente veo en casa. ¿A qué orden pertenecen?

Is there an entrance fee? How much is it?
¿Existe un derecho de entrada? ¿Cuánto es?

While shopping

Vocabulary
mall *centro comercial*
outdoor market *mercado al aire libre*
store *tienda (de)*
supermarket *supermercado*
size *tamano*
clothes *ropa*
French clothes *ropa estilo frances*
Shirt in the local custom (Latin America) *guayabera*
dress *vestido*
skirt *falda*
shirt *camisa*
T Shirt *camiseta*
pants *pantalones*
shorts *pantalones cortos*
underwear *ropa interior*
panties *panty*
girdle/control wear *faja*
brassiere *sostén*
socks *medias* (Latin America) *calcetines* (Spain)
stockings *medias*
shoes *zapatos*
sandals *sandalia, guarache* (MX)
suitcase *maleta*
briefcase *maletín*
back pack *mochila*
computer case *caja de la computadora*

phone carrier *Operadora de teléfono*
chip *SIM*
Wifi *Wifi*
suit *traje*
tuxedo *esmoquin*
formal dress *vestido formal*
track suit *pistatraje*
jewelry *joyería*
bracelet *pulsera*
necklace *collar*
earrings *pendientes*
ring *anillo*
high heels *zapatos de tacón alto*
low heel *tacón bajo*
no heel *sin tacón*
gift *regalo*
candy *caramelo*
souvenir *recuerdo*
watch *reloj*
wallet *cartera* (SP) *billetera* (Lat.Am.)
purse *bolso* (SP) *cartera* (Lat. Am.)
water bottle *cantimplora*
tote bag *bolsón*
home furnishings *muebles para el hogar*
home decor *decoración del hogar*
Red *rojo*
Black *negro*
White *blanco*
Blue *azul*
Yellow *amarillo*
Pink *rosado*
Purple *morado* (m) *púrpura* (f)
Green *verde*
Grey *gris*
Orange *naranja*

How it is said:
How much is this/it?
Cuánto es esto?

Do you have anything on sale? *Tienes algo en oferta?*

I am looking for___.
Estoy buscando _____.

Can you help me?
(Usted) me puede ayudar?

Do you have___?
(Usted) tiene _____?

Are there any ___?
Hay _____?

I'm not sure what it's called in Spanish, but ____.
No estoy seguro/a de lo que se llama en español, pero ___.

I wear size 8.
Yo uso tamaño 8.

I wear shoe size 7.
Uso talla de zapato 7.

Is there a mall here?
Hay un mall aquí?

Do you like flea markets?
Te gustan mercados de pulgas?

Hi. I'm looking for souvenirs.
Hola. Estoy buscando recuerdos.

I would like something unique, that reflects the local culture.
Me gustaría algo único, que refleja la cultura local.

Can you show me souvenirs appropriate for children?
¿Me puede mostrar recuerdos apropiados para los niños?

I brought sundresses with me, but they make me stand out as a tourist.
He traído conmigo vestidos de verano, pero me hacen destacar como un turista.

I'm looking for a pair of dark jeans and a few pastel colored blouses.
Estoy buscando un par de jeans oscuros y unos pocos colores pastel blusas de colores.

I wear size 14.
Me pongo tamaño 14.

I need a pair of fancy sandals to match my new outfit, please. I wear size 8.
Necesito un par de sandalias de lujo para que coincida con mi nuevo equipo, por favor. Puedo usar el tamaño 8.

Do you have a purse to match?
¿Tiene una bolsa para que coincida?

Returns and complaints

How it is said:
The shoes you sold me yesterday, the strap broke a few hours later.
Los zapatos que me vendieron ayer, la correa se rompió un par de horas más tarde

I need a refund, please.
Necesito un reembolso, por favor.

Here is the receipt.
Aquí está el recibo.

I paid on my credit card.
Pagué con mi tarjeta de crédito.

I would prefer a cash refund.
Yo preferiría un reembolso en efectivo.

This hotel room is not the one I requested over the internet.
Esta habitación del hotel no es el que yo pedí en internet.

It has no view of the water.
No tiene ninguna vista del agua.

The air conditioning doesn't work.
El aire acondicionado no funciona.

The refrigerator is warm and there is no water inside.
El refrigerador está caliente y no hay botellas de agua en el interior.

This room is not clean.
Esta habitación no está limpio.

There is a hair on the sheet and a few in the tub.
Hay un pelo en la hoja y unos pocos en la bañera.

I've been charged triple the amount stated for room service. Why?
Me han cobrado el triple de la cantidad declarada de servicio de habitaciones. ¿Por qué?

Expressing Emotion.

Happy – *Feliz*

Sad – *Triste*

Miserable – *Miserable*

Worried – *Preocupado*

Depressed – *Deprimido*

Excited – *Emocionado*

Bored – *Aburrido*

Fed up – *Harto*

Pleased – *Satisfecho*

Delighted – *Encantado*

Surprised – *Sorprendido*

Astonished – *Estupefacto*

Disappointed – *Decepcionado*

Enthusiastic – *Entusiasta*

Relaxed – *Tranquilo*

Stressed – *Estresado*

Anxious – *Ansioso*

Tired – *Cansado*

Exhausted – *Agotado*

Annoyed/Angry – *Enojado*

Furious – *Furioso*

Disgusted – *Asqueado*

Confident – *Seguro*

Sensitive – *Sensible*

Impulsive – *Impulsivo*

Cheerful – *Alegre*

Generous – *Generoso*

Kind – *Amable*

Mean – *Malo*

Crazy – *Loco*

Serious – *Sério*

Honest – *Honesto*

Dishonest – *Deshonesto*

Hard-working – *Trabajador*

Lazy – *Perezoso*

When Ill

I'm sick. I have a headache/stomach ache.

Estoy enferma/o. Tengo un dolor de cabeza/estómago.

I have an allergy.
Tengo una alergia.

Where is the nearest pharmacy?
Dónde está la farmacia más cercana?

He is a diabetic.
Él es diabético.

I need something for diarrhea.
Necesito algo para la diarrea.

She's taking her medicine.
Ella está tomando su medicina.

I have no energy.
No tengo energía.

My back is hurting.
Me duele la espalda.

She needs to go to the emergency room.
Ella tiene que ir a la sala de emergencia.

I see my doctor tomorrow.
Veré mi medico manana.

Prescription (form).
Receta.

Doctor's note/excuse.
Licencia medica.

Sick leave.
Licencia por enfermedad.

I have a problem with my ____.
Tengo un problema con mi_____.

Psychiatrist. *Psiquiatra.*

When visiting the doctor, you might tell him your complaints this way:

I'm very congested.
Estoy muy congestionada.

I'm in a lot of pain.
Tengo mucho dolor.

I've been feeling really tired.
Me he estado sintiendo realmente cansado.

Your doctor will probably respond like this:
How long have you been feeling like this?
Cuánto tiempo se ha sentido así?

Do you have any allergies?
Tiene alguna alergia?

Are you on medication?
Está tomando algún medicamento?

Where does it hurt?
Dónde/Qué le duele?

I am going to take your temperature and blood pressure.
Voy a tomar tu temperatura y la presión arterial

At the theme park.

How to say it.

How much are the tickets?
¿Cuánto son las entradas?

We are foreigners, yes. Is there a different price for tourists?
Somos extranjeros, sí. ¿Existe un precio diferente para los turistas?

What is included in the ticket price?
¿Qué se incluye en el precio del billete?

Are there restaurants and snack bars inside, or should we bring our own lunch?
¿Hay restaurantes y bares en el interior, o debemos llevar nuestra propia comida?

How many rides are there?
¿Cuántos montañas rusas hay?

Are there other attractions?
¿Hay otras atracciones?

How big is the park?
¿Qué tan grande es el parque?

Appendix 1 – Common Verbs

Here are the most commonly used verbs in Spanish and English, with their most commonly used forms. You won't be learning all the forms here, as this book is meant to help you *speak* Spanish, not become a grammarian. I simply don't recommend memorizing verb forms you'll rarely, if ever, use. There are other ways to easily pick up those verb forms up, later on, when you are refining your Spanish by watching movies in Spanish and reading Spanish literature.

A note on formatting: the top of the chart for each verb uses the first person singular to give you an example of how the verb conjugation is translated into English. To understand how the first person plural and the second and third person (singular and plural) are translated, simply substitute the nouns and verb conjugations for "We," "He," "They," etc.

#1 To Be

#1A: Estar - To Be, when the state is changeable

	I am	I was	I used to be	I will be
yo	estoy	estuve	estaba	estaré
tú	estás	estuviste	estabas	estarás
él/ella/Ud.	está	estuvo	estaba	estará
nosotros	estamos	estuvimos	estábamos	estaremos
ellos/ellas/Uds.	están	estuvieron	estaban	estarán

I have been (to Miami) - *He estado (en Miami)*
(Also, see the conjugation of the auxiliary verb, Haber, #6C)

#1B: Ser - To Be, under all other circumstances*

	I am	I was	I used to be	I will be
yo	soy	fui	era	seré
tú	eres	fuiste	eras	serás
él/ella/Ud.	es	fue	era	será
nosotros	somos	fuimos	éramos	seremos
ellos/ellas/U	son	fueron	eran	serán

ds.

I have been (angry)- *He sido (enojado)*
I am being (bad)- *Estoy siendo (malo)*
(Also, see the conjugation of the auxiliary verb, Haber, #6C)

* There is one other example of how to use is/are in Spanish, the word Hay (from Haber), which means "there is/there are," in terms of existence. You will only need to learn this one form, "hay." "Hay" is a quick way to enquire about something which isn't always available. For instance, in some countries, utilities come and go. "Hay luz?" is a quick way to ask your neighbor about electricity. If you've arrived at a small restaurant near closing time, you could ask "Hay comida?" To a fruit vendor, you might ask, "Hay limones?" who might respond, "Si, hay limones aquí."

#2 To Go

#2A: Irse - To Go/Go Out/ Leave

	I'm leaving	I left	I used to go	I would leave (implies "if")	I will leave	Go!/Get out!
yo	me voy	me fui	me iba	me iría	me iré	<not applicable>
tú	te vas	te fuiste	te ibas	te irías	te irás	vete
él/ella/Ud.	se va	se fue	se iba	se iría	se irá	váyase
nosotros	nos vamos	nos fuimos	nos íbamos	nos iríamos	nos iremos	vayámonos, vámonos
ellos/ellas/ Uds.	se van	se fueron	se iban	se irían	se irán	váyanse

So for instance, you would use irse in the following situations:
- I was leaving, but now you have arrived.
- I left before she arrived.
- Let's go!
- They went out to eat.
- They left.

#2B: Ir - To Go, with a particular goal or destination in mind

	I'm going	I went	I used to	I would	I will go	Go!

		go	go			(implies "if")
yo	voy	fui	iba	iría	iré	<not applicable>
tú	vas	fuiste	ibas	irías	irás	ve
él/ella/Ud.	va	fue	iba	iría	irá	vaya
nosotros	vamos	fuimos	íbamos	iríamos	iremos	vayamos
ellos/ellas/Uds.	van	fueron	iban	irían	irán	vayan

I have gone (to bed)- *He ido (a la cama).*
He has gone (shopping) -*Ha ido (a compras).*
(Also, see the conjugation of the auxiliary verb, Haber, #6C)
The verb Ir is particularly useful, because it molds and adapts to other verbs in conversation, so that you don't have to learn too many verb forms. The same way we use "Go" in English, it is used in Spanish, as well.
For instance:
- I'm going to walk. - *Voy a caminar.*
- Are you going to call a taxi? - *Vas a llamar un taxi?*
- He's going to get married. - *Él va a casarse.*

The options are as many as the verbs you can think of to use --and it's common usage to use Ir in this way.

#3 To Be Able - Poder

	I can	I was able to	I would be able to (implies "if")
yo	puedo	pude	podría
tú	puedes	pudiste	podrías
él/ella/Ud.	puede	pudo	podría
nosotros	podemos	pudimos	podríamos
ellos/ellas/Uds.	pueden	pudieron	podrían

#4 To Work - Trabajar

	I work	I worked	I used to work	I will work
yo	trabajo	trabajé	trabajaba	trabajaré
tú	trabajas	trabajaste	trabajabas	trabajarás
él/ella/Ud.	trabaja	trabajó	trabajaba	trabajará
nosotros	trabajamos	trabajamos	trabajábamos	trabajaremos
ellos/ellas/Uds.	trabajan	trabajaron	trabajaban	trabajarán

	Work! (Command)
yo	<not applicable>
tú	trabaja
él/ella/Ud.	trabaje
nosotros	trabajemos
ellos/ellas/Uds.	trabajen

I have worked. -*He trabajado.*
I am working. - *Estoy trabajando.*

#5 To Speak - Hablar

	I speak	I spoke	I was talking (implies "when")	I will speak	Speak!
yo	hablo	hablé	hablaba	hablaré	<not applicable>
tú	hablas	hablaste	hablabas	hablarás	habla
él/ella/Ud.	habla	habló	hablaba	hablará	hable
nosotros	hablamos	hablamos	hablábamos	hablaremos	hablemos
ellos/ellas/Uds.	hablan	hablaron	hablaban	hablarán	hablen

I have spoken. - *He hablado.*
They are speaking. - *Estan hablando.*

#6 To Have

#6A: Tener - To possess, or to need to do something

	I have	I had	I used to have	I would have (implies "if")	I will have
yo	tengo	tuve	tenía	tendría	tendré
tú	tienes	tuviste	tenías	tendrías	tendrás
él/ella/Ud.	tiene	tuvo	tenía	tendría	tendrá
nosotros	tenemos	tuvimos	teníamos	tendríamos	tendremos
ellos/ellas/Uds.	tienen	tuvieron	tenían	tendrían	tendrán

I've had (a cat) - *He tenido (un gato)*
He's having (a struggle) - *Ha tenido (una lucha)*

#6B: Tomar - To Drink (although this verb is usually used for "to take")

	I'll have
yo	tomo
tú	tomas
él/ella/Ud.	toma
nosotros	tomamos
ellos/ellas/Uds.	toman

And to drink? - *A tomar?*
We'll have (coffee) - *Tomamos (café).*

#6C: Haber - To have in the auxiliary sense

	I have	I had
yo	he	había
tú	has	habías

él/ella/Ud.	ha, hay	había
nosotros	hemos	habíamos
ellos/ellas/Uds.	han	habían

#7 To Give

#7A: Dar - To Give

	I give	I gave	I was giving (implies "when")	I would give (implies "if")	I will give
yo	doy	di	daba	daría	daré
tú	das	diste	dabas	darías	darás
él/ella/Ud.	da	dio	daba	daría	dará
nosotros	damos	dimos	dábamos	daríamos	daremos
ellos/ellas/Uds.	dan	dieron	daban	darían	darán

	Give! (Command)
yo	-<not applicable>
tú	da
él/ella/Ud.	dé
nosotros	demos
vosotros	dad

ellos/ellas/Uds.	den

#7B Pasar - To Give (as in To Pass)

	Command: Give (me, her, him ___)
yo	<not applicable>
tú	pasa
él/ella/Ud.	pase

Give me the fan. - *Pasame el abanico.*

#8 To learn - Aprender

	I learn	I learned	I was learning (implies "when")	I would have learned (implies "if")
yo	aprendo	aprendí	aprendía	aprendería
tú	aprendes	aprendiste	aprendías	aprenderías
él/ella/Ud.	aprende	aprendió	aprendía	aprendería
nosotros	aprendemos	aprendimos	aprendíamos	aprenderíamos
ellos/ellas/Uds.	aprenden	aprendieron	aprendían	aprenderían

I will learn

aprenderé

aprenderás

aprenderá

aprenderemos

aprenderán

I am learning. - *Estoy aprendiendo.*
He has learned. - *Ha aprendido.*

#9 To do/make - Hacer

	I make/do	I did/made	I used to make/do	I will make/do
yo	hago	hice	hacía	haré
tú	haces	hiciste	hacías	harás
él/ella/Ud.	hace	hizo	hacía	hará
nosotros	hacemos	hicimos	hacíamos	haremos
ellos/ellas/Uds.	hacen	hicieron	hacían	harán

	Do (it). Make (it).
yo	<not applicable>
tú	haz (lo)
él/ella/Ud.	haga (lo)

What are you doing? - *Qué estás haciendo?*
I have made/ done - *He hecho*

	I have done	I had done	I would have done
yo	he hecho	había hecho	habría hecho
tú	has hecho	habías hecho	habrías hecho
él/ella/Ud.	ha hecho	había hecho	habría hecho
nosotros	hemos hecho	habíamos hecho	habríamos hecho
ellos/ellas/Uds.	han hecho	habían hecho	habrían hecho

Appendix 2: **Pronouns**

-Tackling two pronouns at once.

Spanish pronouns throw most learners off course, because their usage is so different than pronouns in English. In English, the direct and indirect object pronouns always come after the verb. In the following sentence, the direct object, in this case "it," comes right after the verb, and the indirect object "us" follows:

Deborah gave it to us.

Well, in Spanish, for a statement like this (which isn't a command), the direct object pronoun for "it" ("*lo*") and the indirect object pronoun for "us" ("*nos*") are both shifted to the front of the verb. The order of the two pronouns is also reversed --"us" comes first and "it" comes second.

Deborah nos lo dio. (You could think of it like this: Deborah us gave it.)

-An exception.

The next point confused me for a long time. I could never figure out why I was hearing "se lo dio" (substitute whatever verb you like) instead of "le lo dio."

Here is the reason. When both pronouns are similar, as in:

Deborah gave it to her.

Which actually should be "*Deborah le lo dio.*" It is actually said "*Deborah se lo dio.*"

-Using only one pronoun, the direct object.
If there is no indirect object pronoun, the direct object pronoun comes before the verb, as usual.

Tammy took it.
Tammy lo tomó.

-The pronouns themselves.

Indirect Object Pronouns
me: *me*
you: *te*
him/her/it/ formal you: *le*
us: *nos*
them/formal you all: *les*

Direct Object Pronouns
me: *me*
you: *te*
him/her/it/ formal you: *lo/la*
us: *nos*
them/formal you all: *los/las*

Printed in the USA
CPSIA information can be obtained
at www.ICGtesting.com
CBHW061756211024
16187CB00042B/1801